Paula Rego

Paula Rego

SERPENTINE GALLERY

15 October – 20 November 1988

To Victor Willing

Cover:
43 **The Policeman's Daughter** 1987 (detail)
Acrylic on paper/canvas
Saatchi Collection, London

© Copyright the authors and Serpentine Trust 1988

ISBN 1 870814 20 7

Photography by Mário de Oliveira, Christopher Hurst, Irene Rhoden,
Prudence Cuming Associates, Manual Aguiar
Designed by Tim Harvey
Printed by EGA Partnership

As an independent educational charity, the Serpentine Gallery receives
financial support from the Arts Council of Great Britain, and Westminster
City Council. To ensure the gallery is operational throughout the year,
further income needs to be generated from donations, covenants and
sponsorship.

Foreword

To talk of Paula Rego as a late developer may seem inappropriate when one considers the long recognition of her singularity as an artist. She has not wanted critical champions, and the imagery in her work which is most familiar – the animated cast of dogs, monkeys, rabbits, crocodiles – has shown itself unusually potent in its capacity to touch a nerve in common human experience. Yet the series of marvellous paintings completed in the last year or so, and which command the North gallery of the Serpentine, mark in my view a sea-change in her development.

These recent paintings, despite the several disquieting themes which can be read into them, are informed with a solemn, unprotesting quality which argues a newly discovered serenity. In formal terms too there is a stability and an assurance announcing a fresh departure. Such equilibrium, matching rich feeling with a persuasive monumentality, encourages a sense that these pictures are the *early* work of an artist just beginning to realise the full range of her voice.

Paula Rego's paintings have always disclosed secrets. The manner of their disclosure is however no longer secretive. The utterance is more public, confident as well as confiding. Discretion and delicacy are not made casualties of this more assertive stance, nor is there a question of psychological tension being sacrificed as a result of a more deliberate procedure.

Throughout her career Paula Rego has shown herself prepared to confront the vast, parched territory of human misunderstanding. In her earliest works, states of emotional confusion are described by means of expressive drawing and collage; at a later period – the one which up until now has been regarded perhaps as "typical" – through the invention of a boisterous bestiary, allowed licence to wreak a good deal of pictorial havoc. She appears to have become much stricter. A (The?) Devil is still palpable in her recent paintings, but it has been told to behave, allowed as an off-stage presence but not to hog the limelight.

The dislocated and removed sense of time which attaches to the atmosphere of these paintings has prompted some people to read a connection with Balthus and de Chirico. This seems to me to be mistaken. There is nothing voyeuristic about them and their enigmatic quality is not of an oneiric nature. My subjective response is to sense something of Mozart's operas *(Cadet and his Sister)?* and maybe the films of Bertolucci *(Departure)?* Certainly I feel that, in a generalised way, a Mediterranean world is presented. But if her paintings encourage me to thinking of The South it is also in terms of the word's usage in America, implying a state of mind as well as geography, where an emotional and imaginative richness is the partner of a retarded political awareness.

I don't know whether Paula Rego ever read as a child "The Lion, the Witch and the Wardrobe", but the book, if merely in terms of title, has an apt application to her art. Lions and witches make literal appearances in her early work and in *The Family*, the image of a wardrobe plays a crucial role in establishing the possibility of menace in the scene described. However it seems she has discovered a key to unlock the furniture containing her chidhood fears. And in having the courage to use this key she has at the same time become an artist of the first rank.

Alister Warman

Acknowledgements

Contents

The exhibition at the Serpentine emphasises three episodes in Paula Rego's career and is smaller in scale than the recent and much applauded showing of her work in Portugal. London is the beneficiary of a great deal of organisation in Lisbon, and I would like to most warmly thank Dr José Sommer Ribeiro and Maria José Moniz Pereira of the Centro de Arte Moderna, Fundação Calouste Gulbenkian. As well as writing a fine and penetrating essay for the catalogue, Dr Ruth Rosengarten proved an invaluable ally to the project in many other ways and I express my gratitude to her also. The catalogue, which contains a highly readable interview between the artist and John McEwen, is illustrated in colour rather more lavishly than is usual for a Serpentine publication. This has been possible through the generosity of Marlborough Fine Art, where John Erle-Drax has afforded this exhibition his every support.

Without the active collaboration of the artist's mother, Mrs Maria Figueiroa Rego, and of Edward Totah, certain aspects of the exhibition would have been all the harder to realise. We are indebted to them both. The lenders to this show both in Britain and in Portugal are too numerous to mention individually, but I would like to record my appreciation at their generosity in parting with their paintings for such an extended period. Finally I would like to thank Paula Rego for her unwavering commitment to the exhibition during a year of sad personal loss.

ASW
Serpentine Gallery

Inevitable Prohibitions

Even if you cannot immediately recall 'The Virgin spanking the infant Jesus', by Ernst, it will be no surprise to find that it is not paint in search of a subject. Evidently what it is about matters. But this title does give rise to uneasy speculation. In what circumstances could Jesus have deserved chastisement? Could Mary be unjust, or domineering? Ernst's own unease (real or assumed) is apparent in the style which reminds us of the Roman Mannerists, their snooping perspective, sinuous silhouettes, air of menace and always, through disrupted hierarchies, the rumour of plots.

Childhood was full of moments when adult behaviour was perplexing. Were we witness to an act of love or murder? As witness, and not participant, we felt excluded and therefore suspicious. The Mannerist's vision evokes the child's worst fears – looming menace, incomprehensible events, isolation, falling, sudden clamour and broken rules.

However strong our means of outrage in the face of unfairness we knew we were guilty of something – probably curiosity. Innocence is an adult's attribution and refers surely, to the child's lack of knowledge not its lack of guilt. So just as curiosity may have been the first sin, so forbidden knowledge was the most avidly acquired and difficult to forget. We longed to lose that innocence. Secrets and prying were wrapped in excitement. With heat pounding in open mouth they preceded sexual experience, where an intimation of its turmoil and possibly, of other experiences for which we were also unprepared – alarming things like scaling heights, winning prizes and addressing an audience. Yet usually these weren't forbidden even. Erotic ecstacy came later and required, for its achievement, a widespread conspiracy in the prevalent culture to prepare us, yearning for we knew not what as yet unrealised possibility which, then perceived and within grasp, was forbidden.

For those whose education makes little distinction between ethics and etiquette, their imperatives being of equal weight, the world is dangerous. The exemplary young ladies of the Comtesse de Ségur were prepared for an exemplary society and might fall victim – voluptuous and compliant victim – to a latter-day de Valmont.

The romantic is made not born. Made by storytelling, by the precious brevity of life, by wiles and coquetry, by tension and drama – by Art. The limits of experience are not reached by doing what comes naturally. Paula's childhood was well filled with stories and probably she discovered early that humour can disarm the pompous and insincere, leaving the genuinely serious unaffected. Early alarm at the highfalutin' has made her faithful to the world of the popular tale – the versions told before polite society contrived something 'suitable for the children' – which meant the unsophisticated – and told to her by people unaware of Perrault (though very knowing). Of course, 'children' will listen with wide-eyed delight to tales of blood and guts.

Regarding humour, she disappointed some admirers who wanted more, when she decided that some things are not a laughing matter. Wit handles serious matters with a light touch – from a certain fastidiousness perhaps – but that is in the tone of voice, the heart of the matter may be heavy and though nothing can be improved by a long face, even so, to insist always on finding reasons to laugh would betray embarrassment about life's dark side. She has none.

The problem we all have, when confronting those presences emerging from the darkness in or lives, is how to describe them. The truth to which some may be asked to testify, banal facts about rapine and slaughter, are simple by comparison. This more shady truth is complicated by our need to make sense of what we perceive – to give it a form which we ourselves are satisfied is true, which form in turn may even make sense to others – that would be a bonus, but the priority is always our own understanding. Testimony is secondary and if a painter is asked what he means – what he *really* means, by a painting, his answer, if he made one, might still leave us unsatisfied. His understanding is unlikely to have reached an explicable form – in so many words, and may never do so, but a sense of unease has been confronted, which the image has encapsulated, leaving him or her with the feeling that the matter has been settled.

The matter for Paula often concerns domination, or rebellion and domination; or freedom and repression; suffocation and escape. In these dramas her sympathy for the protagonists is ambivalent and wavering – as when she watched a child-prostitute in a fairground whose father stood by as the leering bumpkins sidled past. Who was victim, who exploiter, whore, pimp, or client?

Later in life, the child's games mimicry are bent to adult purposes, but maturity never obliterates our childhood. The image of the child can be that of the 'father of the man' or it may presage an as yet unrealised possibility within us. Paula's girls are both a memory and presentiment.

Ours is a generation which has found it difficult to believe in the inevitability of progress or, consequently, to identify progressives amongst us. The liberal ideal, long central to our values, has been under threat from 'realities', so we have seen *Sturm and Drang,* nostalgia, primitivisms and revivals. The progressive development of the formal means by an avant-garde has paused – any way, it seems, could be forward. The representation of the figure has been a particular embarrassment. Voice of harmony and optimism, the figure does not easily become the imagery of a generation bereft of ideals and making the best of it – guided by expediency, whim and opportunism not principle.

Paula's search for 'a way to do it' is quickly disappointed by renewed dissatisfaction when the image fails to fit the feeling. At an age when most artists advance confidently building on achievement she starts again. In her latest dramas the figures emerge from sullen paint coercing an awkward naturalism; which failure, paradoxically, leads to an uneasy success when after all, this is not prosaic but Gothic in feeling. A lifetime of courting disaster turned around at the last moment – snatching chestnuts from the fire – produces a note of hilarious triumph. It defies the pain.

Victor Willing
London, August 1987

1   **Birthday Party** 1953

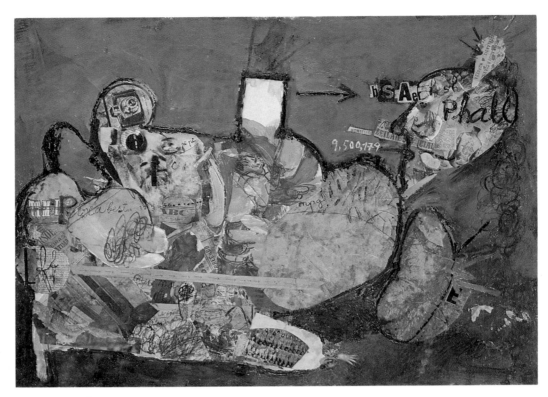

2 **Portrait of a Lady** 1959

3 **The Eating** 1959

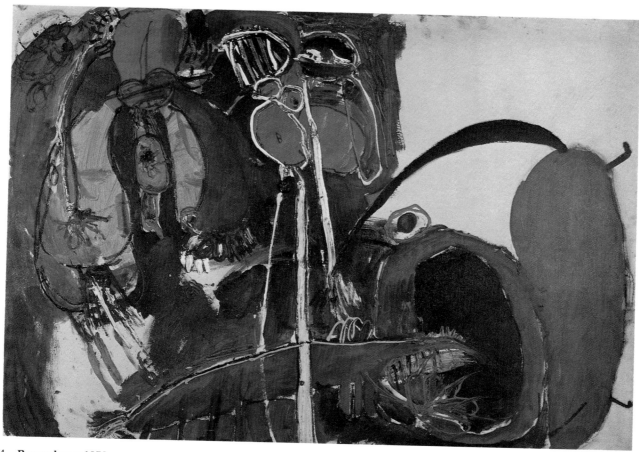

4 **Persephone** 1959

5 **Salazar a Vomitar a Pátria** 1960

7a **Travelling Circus** 1960

7d **Untitled** 1961

7b **Trophy** 1960

7e **Untitled** 1961

7c **Order has been Established . . .** 1961

7f **Long Live Ding-Dong** 1961

7g **Always at your Excellency's Service** 1961

8 **When we had a House in the Country** 1961

9 **Aurora Latina** 1962

12 **Stray Dogs (The Dogs of Barcelona)** 1965

14   **Regicide** 1965

La Règle du Jeu

Paula Rego recalls having played with a miniature Spanish theatre when she was a child. In her recent paintings, young girls enact their moments of privacy or collusion in a three-dimensional space evocative of a stage set (*The Little Murderess, The Maids* – 1987). The analogy with the theatre is a fitting one for Paula's work – within the margins described by the sweep of the stage, the theatre is a platform on which a self-contained world is created, a world with its own rules and logic. The setting of limits within which her imagination might be allowed free reign, runs like a leitmotif through both Paula's works and her statements. The playroom of her childhood was, for her, the first of such spaces, shut off from the threatening outside world and its proscriptions. Her windowless studio, like a playroom, is a self-contained enclosure within the boundaries of which anything is permissible and possible. She often begins her paintings on the floor, kneeling or crouching above them as a child does when at play with her toys. The framing edge of the painting creates the division between fiction and reality, rendering the surface of the painting an arena in which she can enact her terrors and desires, her passion and revenge, without fear of chastisement or censorship. In this area, this enclosed space with its own rules, she can freely tell her stories.

To these analogies – the stage, the playroom – another might be added: the psychoanalyst's consulting room which creates the context, both spatial and temporal, for the uninhibited telling of one's story, the story of one's life. Within the bounds of the analyst's room, the patient's fantasies and realities interweave in the unfolding of his or her narrative. More significant than what "actually" happened is the telling of the tale, or, more precisely, the event is only accessible through its telling, that which springs to mind in its unravelling. The process of Paula's picture-making is a comparable one. In the collages of the 1960s and '70's, the painted images are subjected to cutting, mutilation, overpainting and rearrangement through which the story emerges. In 1981, collage is abandoned in favour of painting directly, but the procedure is analogous: the painting is considered to have been completed when the story has been told. While this story is not to be equated with a literal, verbal narrative, the artist never allows her brush to meander aimlessly, unmediated and dictated to by the unconscious alone, for however fluid, it is always a determined, conscious, intelligent line. The story, however, is entirely dependent on the manner of its telling, on the precise graphic quality of the drawing, on the process itself. "I watch the stories appear," she tells us. Overpainting replaces cutting and glueing, until the image is "just right", until the form corresponds to the idea with a disconcerting precision.

In Paula Rego's work, a tension is established between outer and inner worlds. Her recent interview with John McEwen elucidates the way in which external suggestions and internal needs work upon each other, the locus of intersection between reality and desire. Turning points in her work have frequently resulted from this crossing of inner need with outer suggestion, and it is in this light that we should see the impact on her work of the 1959 Dubuffet exhibition at the ICA; her abandonment of collage in 1981 at the suggestion of a friend; her fascination with *The Realms of the Unreal* (a strange narrative in thirteen volumes written and illustrated by a cleaner in a Chicago hospital, Henry Darger, and featuring the Vivian Girls on whom she loosely based her eponymous series of paintings in 1984); the importance of the "Northern Lights" exhibition in London in 1986. Similarly, when the artist was casting about for "stories" in 1981, her late husband, the painter Victor Willing, happened to recall a toy theatre he had had as a child, with its three characters – a monkey, a bear and a one-eared dog. These images, as well as a Spanish newspaper-cartoon series about the vicissitudes in the daily life of a husband and wife, together provided the springboard for which she was searching, resulting in pictures dealing with guilt and jealousy, power and passion. Work such as *Red Monkey beats his Wife* (1981), *Wife cuts off Red Monkey's Tail* (1981) and *Chicken persuading Woman* deal baldly with the competitive and coercive aspects of triangular relationships.

The analogy between Paula Rego's work and the processes of psychoanalysis is not a fortuitous one. Psychoanalysis teaches us that maturity never obliterates our childhood. Memory acts as a bridge between what we once were and what we are now, and thus serves as the cornerstone for the unfolding of the narrative – not only that which is immediately recollected, but also that which springs to mind apparently unbeckoned, that which prevails itself only in slips of the tongue or lapses, that which must gradually be coaxed into consciousness. Even a hasty perusal of this exhibition will reveal Paula's obsession with memory as the medium through which her ideas are given body. Her childhood is recollected not as a series of distant events from which she as an adult is disconnected, but rather as always present, more or less accessible in the here and now, waiting to be tapped, colouring the incidents that affect her today. The fears of the adult – the dark, the inscrutable boundlessness of nature – are continuous with those of the child, even if now harnessed. Indeed, harnessed by the act of painting itself. "I paint," she told Alberto de Lacerda in 1965, "to give fear a face"[1]. Bringing the shadowy phantoms to light, she is better able to scrutinize, analyse and tame them. The sureness of her drawing, what John McEwen calls her "innate sense of design", her natural flair for composition, subject these fears to aesthetic control and ensure that they do not spill out, formless and incomprehensible.

Tirelessly drawn up from the well of childhood, there is a persistence of themes and concerns which insinuate themselves through Paula's various stylistic metamorphoses. Victor Willing, her most astute and lyrical critic, once observed that two of the predominant themes in her work were time past and domination.[3] To these might be added the themes of nurturing and punishment, freedom and repression, power and impotence, as well as the disjunction between what the self desires and what the social order prescribes or what reality has to offer. In *The Bride* (1985), the young girl coyly embroiders her trousseau, dreaming of her wedding night, when she will ride her fierce dragon of a husband. Moving to the bottom left of the painting, we share the marital reality with her as she coaxes the rising tail of a benevolent and somewhat embarrassed crocodile.

These themes are characteristically interwoven one with the other. Images of domination and authority of all sorts persist – whether spiritual *(Annunciation, 1980)*, political *(Salazar a Vomitar a Pátria of 1959, When we had a House in the Country, 1961, Stray Dogs, 1965)* or the domestic dominion of little tyrants and petty despots, invariably male *(Red Monkey beating Wife, Red Monkey offers Bear Poisoned Dove 1981, Chicken persuading Woman, 1982)*. The subversive power of angry or simply fed-up women, who, like Breughel's "Dulle Griet" are prepared to march into hell, also plays its part here *(Wife cuts off Red Monkey's Tail 1981 The Little Murderess, 1987)*. The concern with relationships of power is also evident in a gutsy delight which the artist takes in making some of her characters give "lessons" to others – make-up, sewing and dancing lessons in which the imparting of knowledge empowers those already initiated. The cadet's sister too (*The Cadet and his Sister*, 1988) attempts to introduce him to the mysteries of female sexuality, but his real lesson, the artist tells us, is to accept the fact of his impotence.

In the series entitled *Girl with Dog* of 1986, the themes of domination, of nurturing and punishment, are handled with great subtlety. In the works of the early 1980's, animals and vegetables stand in as substitutes for human beings with all their foibles and pride, anger and tenderness, cruelty and guile. In the *Girl and Dog* series, however, the dogs are pets, the domesticated and ultimately impotent charge of the girls who administer food, medicine, grooming and attention, their tenderness masking their real power. Nowhere is this more poignantly felt that in *Girl shaving Dog*, where the dog's safety, as he submissively extends his neck to the blade, is entirely dependent on the girl's patience and clemency. Throughout Paula Rego's work, the instruments of cooking and cosmetics – those which are traditionally wielded in the domestic space by women – are also the agents of multilation and amputation (*Pioneers, Rabbit and weeping Cabbages, Cabbage and Potato*, 1982, *The Little Murderess*, 1987). The dividing line between nurturing and harming – between love and murder – is always hair-thin, for the artist's concern is not with good and evil at their extremes, but with the area between, the acts of cruelty with which love is shot.

Although they never preach a moral lesson, refusing to take sides as to who is good or bad, right or wrong, the scenarios of these works clearly unfold in a moral universe. Here, the playroom imposes its own rules, overlapping with the world of the fairytale, the popular story, the comic-book and cartoon-strip. Paula admits her debt not only to the caricatures of Pluma y Lapis, the cartoons of Walt Disney, and the drawings of Benjamin Rabier and English illustrators such as Tenniel, Gilray, Rowlandson and Rackham, but also to a verbal narrative tradition, whether written or spoken: the tales of Perrault, Beatrix Potter and the Comtesse de Ségur, Arthurian legends, Portuguese folk tales, the yarns spun by her grandmother or Aunt Ludgera. As a story told by adults to children, and then by those children, when grown up, to their own children, the fairytale not only enters the respository of collective memory, but also acts as a meeting point between the world of the adult and that of the child. It serves to mediate, for the child, between apparent inequalities: between generations (adults and children), classes (the prince and the pauper or the king and the shepherd) and genders. This mediation is effected by a strategy of reversal[4] through which inequality is overcome and hierarchies are toppled. The world of the fairytale – as of many a cartoon – is one in which the moral order of polite society, hypocritical or merely incomprehensible from the standpoint of the child, is upturned.

This strategy of reversal has a long history in popular culture, in "fools' feasts", carnivals, burlesque and travesty[5]. It has its literary and visual equivalents in such images as "the ship of fools" or "the upside down world", both of which first appeared in the mediaeval period. Popular prints depicting the "upside down world" show fish angling a man out of the ocean where birds swim, while a boat glides on land, fish twitter in the trees, an ox slices open a person and a dog trains a human being to fetch a stick. Our own world is ruled by a pecking order which runs: God – Man – Dog: "Why not let the dog to the beating for a change?" Paula asks.

In Paula Rego's paintings, morality is imposed from the outside in the form of prohibitions which, making no inner sense to the characters, are subverted in all manner of pranks. The dog indeed does the beating. While *real life* demands good behaviour – for "one must survive", Paula notes – the painting becomes the legitimate arena in which the artist might freely enact her anarchic or self-destructive fantasies: the lover is hanged (*Martyrs*, 1967), a pompous, speechifying potato cuts off his own nose (*Cabbage and Potato*, 1982), and the Vivian girls break Paula's mother's valuable china tea-service. The morality imposed by society concerns itself not only with the ethics of Christianity and the catechism it teaches its children, but also with modes and manners, with the rules of polite behaviour – one must drink from the finest porcelain and wear white gloves when visiting Lisbon. Paula loves to play on the edge – she loves to wear the white gloves, but she also derives a special, rebellious pleasure from taking them off when she's not quite supposed to.

Despite frequent comparison to Hieronymous Bosch, her garden of earthy delights is not a world of moral absolutes, of thou shalts and thou shalt nots in which the characters are ultimately answerable to some superior being, but a secular world of petty, mundane "sins" – collusion and conspiracy (*Prey, Two girls and a Dog*, 1986), secrets (*The Pig's Secret*, 1984), revenge (*Wife cuts off Red Monkey's Tail*) and jealousy (*Red Monkey beats Wife*, 1981). While the artist's critical eye is not devoid of compassion, there is no spiritual reward serving as a corrective to temptation. Most significantly, absolutes are replaced by ambivalence. This is especially the case in the most recent paintings. In *Prey* (1986), for instance, we are never quite sure who or what the prey is. Similarly in *Two Girls with Dog* (1987), we seem to be about to witness some unspeakable act, or perhaps not . . . and how are we to interpret the grim determination with which the policeman's daughter, in her cinch-waisted white dress, polishes her father's erect black boot? (*The Policeman's Daughter*, 1987). This ambivalence is a product not only of the moment depicted, but also of the drawing itself. The artist remarks that, ironically, the more precisely she captures a gesture, the greater its ambiguity, and the wider its scope for multiple readings[6]. We are constantly invited to re-view and reconsider.

The anarchic spirit with which laws are transgressed is manifest not only in the content of the paintings, but also in the process of their making. Paula Rego's works oppose the expressionist and heroic. The pompous self-importance of the grand gesture is most frequently a characteristic of her male characters such as the Red Monkey. She claims that "life is full of men making a grand gesture and falling on their arse"[7]. One might say that the entire historiography of western art, if not its history, has until recent times, been a series of heroic, grand gestures. The "small gestures" of the illustrators, cartoonists and story-tellers which Paula loves, are all, significantly, outside the mainstream of "High Art".

This historiography is underpinned by one predominant metaphor – that of paternity. The argument runs thus: a mother is always unquestionably connected to her child in a link of causality, of continuity and contiguity. The power to create and lay claim to posterity, to pass down a name, is, however, granted by social contract to the father. In James Joyce's *Ulysses*, Stephen Dedalus remarks that paternity is a "legal fiction" invented by man. Since a man cannot verify his fatherhood, paternity is a tale he tells himself to claim possession of the child, an invocation conferring certainty upon the uncertain. In the *Odyssey*, Homer puts in Telemachus's mouth the words, "My mother certainly says I am Odysseus's son; but for myself I cannot tell. It's a wise child that knows its own father"[8]. Put graphically, the Red Monkey, suspecting the child is not his, beats the wife in impotent rage, for he will never really know. The father is the mediating term between the closed mother-child dyad and society at large, and as such, the Name of the father is the third term which intrudes upon this closed dyadic relation, introducing the social and symbolic order. Over the father's relation to his offspring, there always hangs a question mark, and it is by the symbolic act of granting upon the child a name, his name, that the father legitimises the child, makes it "his".

The history of western art is written in diachronic, genealogical terms, one style begetting the next. The artists "stamps" his progeny – painting or sculpture – with his legitimating mark which is his touch, his personal style, his name. Not only anonymously produced crafts such as embroidery and ceramics, but also illustration and cartoon, all lie outside this genealogy of serious High Art, its illegimitate children. This tradition of High Art, embodying in some fundamental way a Law, was experienced by Paula Rego as a constraint, a kind of "punishment room". The discovery of Dubuffet and Henry Miller in 1959 freed her from these strictures, showing her that the raunchy, humorous elements usually considered unsuited to serious art, were not taboo, that the scribbles of children or the obsessive doodling of madmen could serve as models for "real" painting. The interest in non-hegemonic forms of art has remained a constant in her work. This is manifest in her adoption first of collage and then of a variety of graphic styles, not adhering to any single one and using them undiluted in her work, thus eschewing the notion of style as signature or self-expression. In her latest paintings, it is Tenniel's *Alice* and the illustrations from the catechism of her childhood that are evoked. As the artist herself has perceptively remarked, it is, ironically, when she releases herself from the constraints of High Art, "by not trying to do art", that she makes her best pictures.

As Paula has gained assurance, these conscious strategies have become absorbed into her working method. It would be fruitless fo search for the exact source or "meaning" of her images in the extensive range of popular materials she uses, as these have become enmeshed with the "stories" of her own past. Indeed, images from the collective past and those from one's personal past tend for all of us to unite into a single narrative thread. From the moment we acquire language, we are steeped in narrative which, as Michel Butor has pointed out, takes the most varied forms: "from family tradition, or the news we exchange at dinner about what we have done during the day, to journalistic reports of historical works"[9] A memory from childhood, a popular tale, a lesson from the catechism, an opera, a news item, an incident seen on a street corner, a domestic conflict – all these unite to form a single narrative thread which weaves in and out of Paula's paintings. *The Birthday Party* (1953) is a witty pastiche of a monumental painting by the Portuguese 19th century painter Columbano Bordalo Pinheiro; *Stray Dogs* (1965) was painted after the artist read a news item about the municipal authorities of Barcelona solving the problem of stray dogs by strewing the streets with poisoned meat; *Regicide* (1965) seems to relate directly to the assassination of King Carlos I of Portugal and his son, who in February 1908 were shot while driving in a carriage in Lisbon. While such anecdotes feed into the paintings, the mingling of the real and imagined, the borrowed and recollected, the funny and the cruel – and indeed the desired and the dreaded – prevent the "stories" from being simple illustrations.

This new assurance has also led the artist, over the past year or so, to dare to drop the mask provided by the animals, and, in the very latest paintings, to introduce "boy" characters for the first time. The earlier "horror vacui" has given way to a clearer emptier space, a wide, low-slung horizon with overtones of Metaphysical Painting, emphasised by the chalkier, more muted palette[10]. She has even, on occasion, overridden the agoraphobia of the earlier works and ventured outdoors, out of the safety of the playroom. But, when it is not merely a simulated exterior, a painted theatrical backdrop, it is a space very much shaped by human beings, an enclosure or extension of their indoor spaces: the terrace, the patio, the little garden, perhaps a nearby beach. The packed solidity of the figures which people these scenarios, their monumentality, imbues them with an unsettling presence and seriousness.

These paintings have elicited numerous comparisons with the work of Balthus. But while Balthus's peeping glimpses into rooms – where pubescent girls sleep in voluptuous abandon, lounge about stroking cats, play cards or undress – are unmistakable expressions of a male fantasy of burgeoning female sexuality, Paula's girls are seen with the eye and memory of a woman. There is no idealisation, no playing to a hidden male spectator. The girls are ponderous, and seem to have long lost their innocence. They speak eloquently, if quietly, of sensuality, connivance, guilt and solitude as experienced by the female characters. Paula herself has stated that she does not wish to be considered as a "woman artist"[11] – which in effect, would mean being relegated to the sidelines, outside the mainstream. However, it goes without saying that sexual differentiation is written into the process and rules of socialisation – not only parental admonitions to good behaviour or the chastisement of her wicked teacher Violeta, in Paula's case, but also, in a more general sense, into the very acquisition of language. Her experience as a human being is inseparable from her experience as a woman. Ever observant, analytical, subversive, it is to this experience in all its rich diversity that Paula Rego's work addresses itself.

Ruth Rosengarten
Lisbon 1988

I wish to express my gratitude to João de Pina Cabral, Patricia Morris and Maria de Lourdes Lima dos Santos for their helfpul and interesting comments on this text.

[1] Alberto de Lacerda, *Fragmento de um poema intitulado Paula,* exhibition catalogue, Sociedade Nacional de Belas Artes, Lisbon, 1965.

2 Victor Willing – "The Imagiconography of Paula Rego", *Colóquio,* April 1971, p. 49).

[3] Ibid.

[4] Michel Butor. "On Fairy Tales", in *Inventory,* Jonathan Cape, London, 1970.

[5] See Jacques Heers: *Fêtes de fous et carnavals,* Fayard, Paris, 1983.

[6] Paula Rego in Alexandre Melo and João Pinharanda: "Paula Rego: Tudo quanto pinto vem de Portugal", *Jornal de Letres, Artes e Ideias,* Lisbon, 15 de Junho, 1987.

[1] In Victor Willing, *Paula Rego,* Catalogue for exhibition at Arnolfini, Bristol and Galerie Espace, Amsterdam 1983.

[8] Homer: *The Odyssey,* Book I.

[9] Michel Butor: "The novel as research", op. cit. p. 26.

[10] See Lynne Cooke: "Paula Rego", *Flash Art,* no. 134, May 1987, pp. 90-91.

[11] In conversatioan with the author. See also Maria José Mauperin: "Paula Rego: As crianças gostam desta violência", *Expresso,* 3 April 1982, p. 28.

15 **Red Monkey beats his Wife** 1981

17 **Red Monkey offers Bear a Poisoned Dove** 1981

16   **Wife cuts off Red Monkey's Tail** 1981

18   **The Bear, The Bear's Wife and Son play with The Red Monkey** 1981

20 **Pregnant Rabbit telling her Parents** 1982

21 **Rabbit and weeping Cabbage** 1982

24　**Samurai** 1982

28   **The Girl of the Golden West** 1983

29   **The Pig's Secret** 1984

30　**On the Beach** 1985

31 **The Bride** 1985

32   **Untitled 'Girl & Dog' series** 1986

33   **Untitled 'Girl & Dog' series** 1986

34   **Untitled 'Girl & Dog' series** 1986

35   **Untitled 'Girl & Dog' series** 1986

Untitled 'Girl & Dog' series 1986

Untitled 'Girl & Dog' series 1986

36   Untitled 'Girl & Dog' series 1986

37   **Girl lifting up her Skirts to a Dog** 1986

38　**Prey** 1986

Sleeping 1987 collection: Arts Council of Great Britain

40 **The Little Murderess** 1987

39 **Two Girls and a Dog** 1987

Snare 1987 collection: The British Council

41   **Looking Back** 1987

Paula Rego

in conversation with John McEwen

JM: What is your first memory?

PR: I don't have one first memory. I can remember always playing on my own. I had no brother or sisters, so I was stuck up there in this playroom.

JM: This was in Lisbon?

PR: First of all we lived in Lisbon, then we moved to Estoril because I had the beginnings of TB. This was when I was three. My parents had been to England to stay for a while, because my father, who was an engineer, was working over here, and I got this infection in the lungs. But I loved my grandmother's house in Lisbon. It was wonderful because I was allowed to go to the kitchen, you see.

JM: Your weren't allowed to do this at home?

PR: No, no.

JM: You went to the kitchen . . .

PR: I went to the kitchen and there were dead chickens and cooking and people ironing and just everything. It was centre of activity, which I liked very much. And my grandmother was very good to me. She told me stories and didn't leave me alone in the dark, so I wasn't afraid there at all. And my grandfather spoiled me. He gave me lots of toys. He used to get me toys sent from Germany specially, vast big bears and dolls. But at Estoril I first was aware of the outdoors, something outside the house, and I was absolutely terrified. My mother said I was afraid of the flies. I was afraid of everything. I couldn't bear to be put outside and I was afraid of children. Oh God, it was awful. It was just terror, terror.

JM: It still affects you, obviously?

PR: It's very important. The influence of paintings, all that stuff, that's fifth on the list. The most important thing of all is the early period which I'm still living now.

JM: There's not much sense of outdoors in your pictures.

PR: That's right. I don't like landscape. Even in England if I walk in a park, I always feel I'm being followed. I don't feel one with nature at all. I don't like it. That's why I like the city because it's like a big house, like being indoors all the time.

JM: Were you strictly brought up?

PR: Yes I was. I had a girl who looked after me and I had to eat all this porridge which I loathed, and there were so many things that were forbidden. Everything was clouded in some mystery. You didn't walk through the house at ease; you just felt there were monsters everywhere, even in your bedroom. My grandfather once gave me a little doll just like a real baby, made of flesh-like rubber. And I cut its little fingers off. I remember the thrill of sitting there on the floor with the scissors and cutting first the little thumb, then the middle one . . .

JM: Struwelpeter?

PR: No, I didn't have that as a kid.

JM: Why do you think you did it then?

PR: I didn't like it. It was too much like a real baby, I think. I don't remember how I thought at the time except the pleasure of cutting the fingers off and my mother coming in and saying: 'Oh, what are you doing ruining that beautiful present!' But she wasn't cross. I think she understood.

JM: So you weren't given a smack.

PR: No, I never got smacked for anything. I was very well brought up and I always did exactly as I was told.

JM: But inside your head you were up to no good.

PR: Well, this is it. This is what I always say to students: your freedom, our freedom, is here. We have total freedom to paint exactly what we please. Exactly. It doesn't hurt anybody. Scaredy cat! I still am. I like taking risks in painting, painting on the edge, but I'm very careful in real life. You have to survive, don't you.

JM: Your imagination was allowed full scope because you were very much on your own.

PR: Total, total. I mean I was in this playroom with my toys for hours and hours on end and very few people came in there . And I used to do a lot of drawings. I used to sit on the floor and make this aaaaaaaaaaa noise, I still do it when I draw now, and I still draw on the floor. Most of the time I'm unaware I'm making a noise, obviously, but I know it still gives me the same satisfaction it always did. My mother knew I was alright when she could hear this noise. She didn't have to come in. And for me being in this studio, working in this studio where we are now, is exactly like being in that playroom when I was five. That kind of childhood, where you're stuck in a room all day, is the best training for a painter.

JM: And yet it must be a bit different?

PR: Obviously it's different. One is more aware of what goes on because, you know, the dramas that are played out here have to do with the later developments. A lot of what goes on in these pictures is to do with pubescent girls. That comes later than when you're five. So, I'm more aware but I'm still playing games with the characters; and I'm still sitting on the floor to draw and paint. I start all these big paintings on the floor. I find it intimidating to have the thing up on the wall looking back at me. I'm not in control. So they go on the wall when I'm about half way through.

JM: What about school? Was that a release or a distraction?

PR: I had a teacher at home whom I loathed with every pore in my body. I loathed her. She was rough and cruel and used to hit me. She taught me for two and a half years, so I could do my Portuguese exams. And I used to be so terrified. I used to be literally sick from fear of her. We'd go up to my playroom and she'd give me the lessons there. And she was horrible. She used to say 'You can't draw. You'll never be able to draw.' But being a child I never told my mother, because that was how I thought it was meant to be. If my mother came in I'd think: 'Please stay! Please stay!'. Then when I was 10 or so I went to this English School, St Julian's. It was my first school really and I was terrified, but very soon I got used to it and I loved it. I liked sports particularly.

JM: Was God any comfort? I presume religion came into your childhood a lot?

PR: Not much. Not much, because my father was not religious. My mother was. She went to Mass, but my father if anything was anti-priest. He was what in Portugal would be called a 'good liberal' – rather an old-fashioned notion but that's what he was. The Church was very powerful there, very repressive. So, I wasn't allowed to go to church really. I mean I didn't go to church. No. But one of the lessons at kids' school was catechism and then it was frightening really. The worst nightmare I've ever had in my life was from the catechism, where they said if you left the door half open the Devil would come and get you in the night. And I did, and I dreamt the Devil came and got me and I was terrified. In the new paintings I've tried to get some of the clarity of the catechism illustrations, which were very clearly drawn and printed in basic colours. So religion to me was scary. And because of Fatima you were very conscious of miracles. My mother's friends gave me saints and rosaries and things, which I put in a drawer by my bed to protect me, like magic. It wasn't proper religion.

JM: Nonetheless you have been brought up with a strong idea of good and evil.

PR: The manners and rules of a bourgeois society, which is what we lived in, were far more important than matters of conscience. Like you must always wear white gloves when you go to Lisbon, that was very important. So lying was one of the things one did a lot.

JM: But wouldn't you agree that the people in your pictures know they're often getting up to no good?

PR: There's a smirk somewhere.

JM: But there's a conflict too, isn't there?

PR: I don't think anything like Faust, no. It's nothing to do with good and evil at the roots. It's to do with half things. To do with cheating, lying, the half-sins, the mediocre ones.

JM: But you still call them 'sins', which seems quite indicative.

PR: Well there isn't another word for it really. I suppose it's to do with how people behave rather than philosophical questions.

JM: And you don't take sides?

PR: I observe. It's very difficult to take sides, isn't it? You have to sort out what's important and I've always been very bad at that, even in précis lessons at school I always picked out what wasn't important. I've always been very bad at rounding off and making sense of things. That's why Vic was so helpful to me because he did that for me.

JM: What about Art? Did that come into your childhood much?

PR: My mother had been to art school. She was there only six months as a girl but she had a great deal of flair and she has always had a very good eye for painting. But she always says: 'I never encouraged you', which I think is true. There were art books in the house. My father bought me books on art when he saw that was what I was interested in. He bought me a book on Dada and Surrealism when I was fourteen. It was like a story book to me, looking at those pictures was just wonderful. It wasn't a revelation because it was just like a book of fairy stories. It didn't amaze me at all. It was what I was used to. And he used to take me to the opera. He had a box in the theatre in Lisbon. He had a record of 'Carmen' and he played it over and over again, the opera, and taught me all about it before he took me to see it as a surprise. I must have been thirteen. I think that's what was important about the opera. I became more involved with my father. This has been the story of my life. I'm very easily influenced.

JM: You must have seen films too.

PR: I saw 'Snow White and the Seven Dwarfs', which was just like discovering the world for me. I must have been tiny. My grandmother used to get a box in the cinema with Luzia, that's my grandmother's maid. We used to go there and we used to take a picnic – Berlin Balls – a sort of doughnut – and cakes. That was the best treat I could have in the whole world. They were very partial to Carmen Miranda in Portugal, so I was taken to see her – and 'Pinocchio', 'The Wizard of Oz', Fred Astaire. It was just wonder-ful. I still love the movies now, much more than the theatre or the opera. They take you right out of yourself. I love Buñuel. I think the greatest shock I ever had was when I saw 'Los Olvidados'. And Nicholas Roeg. His films are always beautiful to look at and they have that peculiar light.

JM: And do you feel films have influenced you?

PR: A great deal, particularly the Disney ones.

JM: In what way?

PR: Well, they're so sinister, particularly the early ones were very spooky. 'Snow White' has the bit where the step-mother changes into a witch, becomes an ugly woman with a big nose and warts – that's a very, very frightening bit. I think all children are scared there. Pinocchio was scary because it seems to take part in a world which is below the other worlds. Well, it actually takes part inside the whale, part of it. It's a very dark film, lots of shadows and bits you can't see. I found that very unpleasant.

JM: Tell me a bit about fairy stories. They were told to you in childhood and you studied them as part of a professional project in 1976. Are there big differences between English and Portuguese ones? You once told me you thought the mistiness of England had had an effect on our children's literature. It's softer, more fond of mystery.

PR: English or Portuguese, they come from pretty much the same source. Portuguese ones are slightly cruder. The Portuguese don't like nature. They cut down the trees – not now so much, but they used to – shoot all the birds, kick the dog. Not very kind, and this is in the stories. They're more brutal, more peasant-like than English ones, where there's more mysticism, more love of nature.

JM: But you were told a lot of stories, weren't you? People like your grandmother told you stories rather than reading them from books.

PR: The summer holidays were always spent at my grand-mother's house in the countryside at Ericeire, and that was a very interesting set up. Ludgera, my old aunt, used to come and stay there and she was an extraordinary person. She was tragic – her daughter had died and her husband had died – but she was always full of fun. She'd come in dis-guises. She used to arrive dressed up as a hobo pretending to be drunk, brandishing a bottle. She called this person Piolho, which roughly means the 'louse', the 'nit'. She dres-sed up to amuse us, not for any kinky reason. And she used to tell me stories non-stop. She used to make up stories according to what I wanted to hear, you see. We'd sit under the eucalyptus tree after my siesta and she'd say: 'What shall we tell the story of today?' And I'd say, 'Let's have the king with the daughter who was very wicked', that kind of thing; and she would elaborate the story according to my demands on and on, from day to day. I just sat there and listened. It was a most delicious feeling. She was the best. But there was also my grandmother and an old servant of my mother's, who used to come and sit in my bedroom at night, because I was so frightened of the dark, and tell me stories from her country, the country place she came from, till I fell asleep. She'd tell me rustic stories about animals – the ant that eats the belly of the goat, the rabbit's revenge. She was very old, maybe ninety, and I loved her stories as well.

JM: Did you do a lot of dressing up?

PR: I loved playing with the beautiful little toy theatre my father had as a child, a Spanish theatre. I used to put little plays on. And I took it out again after my last show and restored it and it was then I thought 'I want to do something like that now in my pictures'. Actually for the Genet picture, 'The Maids', I went to Harrods and bought some doll's house furniture to make a little set, not to illustrate but to get my mind working. It served to set a mood.

JM: But these latest paintings are very precise about clothes, and you always dress with a lot of style.

PR: My grandfather used to show me off to his friends. I had to perform and get dressed up, smartened up, in frocks, very pretty frocks, which I loved, and little coats, things that had been bought specially for me. Tyrolean clothes were fashionable and tartan skirts and pinafores. I sometimes find myself putting these clothes I wore on the girls in my pictures now. I use pinafores a lot. Clothes enclose the body and tighten it and give you a feeling of wholeness. You are contained inside your clothes. So I put them in the pictures, and people from that time too sometimes. The girl holding the man in 'The Family' is my little cousin Manuela, it's exactly her portrait. She was very important for me. She was five years younger but I played a lot with her in the sun, at the seaside, which was always very important to me – the beach and the sea. We lived by the sea in Estoril.

JM: But she's much older in the picture.

PR: She's big because she's got to be bigger than the man, but her look is as I remember it when she was about eight.

JM: And the shoes are quite specific too.

PR: The shoes, I don't like them so much. I have a bit of a shoe fetish, though not so much any more either. Shoes are bloody difficult to do. Then you know it's not so nice because they're always eating the socks. You know that feel-

ing when you're a kid and your socks are always being eaten by the shoes.

JM: Does the horrible teacher come in?

PR: She appears all the time. I've done drawings of her, but she hasn't got into a painting yet. I haven't dared do that. She's the spirit of evil. In the recent pictures my model for a lot of the figures has been Lila, not my cousin but the other Lila, who lives with us and helped me look after Vic – who needed a lot of looking after in those days, with his multiple sclerosis.

JM: What books made an impression on you as a child?

PR: I loved the English illustrators.

JM: Have they influenced you at all?

PR: Oh very much. Tenniel, especially his 'Alice in Wonderland' drawings, is a particular favourite.

JM: I suppose there's a whiff of him in the latest, large, paintings.

PR: Yes, I think so. His characters are extremely well defined, which I like. But there's Arthur Rackham, Beatrix Potter, lots and lots of other English illustrators I like the look of. And not just English ones, of course. In fact, curiously, because my mother's upbringing had been French I had more French books as a child than English. I loved Benjamin Rabier's drawings, for instance. He was the man who drew that advertisement, 'La vâche qui rit'. And there were the adventures of a dog and a goose, Gedeon and Placide. I loved them.

JM: Portugal has such a long history of association with England – were your parents very Anglophile?

PR: Very much so. They wanted me brought up in an English way, so I went to an English school in Portugal, St Julian's, from the age of ten, took my School Cert, so I had English qualifications. A very happy memory is the jingle of the BBC World Service, which my father used to listen to every night. I could hear it from my bedroom; it's still a wonderful sound to me. But I must say at St Julian's we had very good art teachers. They really were very encouraging. I got a lot of prizes and I think it was that encouragement that made me want to make it a full-time thing. I met one of them recently, Mr Sarsfield.

*   *   *

JM: And then you went to the Slade. What was that like?

PR: I didn't know what it was, it was so weird, dark and bohemian. After Portugal it was quite alarming again.

JM: Did you find your voice as a painter there?

PR: Not till much later. At the Slade I began by painting these disgusting pictures of cities in flames with everybody screaming, running away – terribly over the top. And, can you imagine, I thought they were very good. They were terrible, really awful. And people said 'Oh you can't do something you don't know about', and of course they were right. I knew something about cities in flames. And I learned how to draw a bit, you know. But I spent most of my time doing these pictures from my head, which was encouraged. Not a restricting art school at all. Bloody good it was. And the subjects we were given for the summer comps – we had a set subject every year – were things like The Raising of Lazarus; you know, things to do from your head. They encouraged that.

JM: Do you remember specific teachers?

PR: Willy Townsend was my tutor there and he was very encouraging. I remember very, very much enjoying talking to Lowry, of all people. He said: 'I couldn't do that. That's really very good.' I have a very soft spot for him because of that, because he was so nice to me; though I don't really like his pictures that much, no. And then I had a bad time with Victor Pasmore. He was difficult. He was very rude to me. So you see, you got very conflicting opinions.

JM: Above all, you met your husband Victor Willing there. Now he was a big Slade star at that time, wasn't he.

PR: We met when I was seventeen. Well, my dear, it was just like a blow on the head. He really was a star, yes. He was my god – smart, intelligent, handsome, talented, the whole caboozle. He was seven years older and married, what's more. It was very frightening for me really because it was just too much. And I was very shy. I didn't speak in those days.

JM: But you were a star too. You won prizes.

PR: Well 'Under Milkwood' was set up as a summer project in 1954. The first prize was divided and I shared it with David Storey. The only other picture I have from art school is 'The Birthday Party'. 'The Birthday Party', especially, is ambitious. It's big or at least was big for those days. I thought it might be interesting to show an early picture because in a funny way they connect with the most recent ones, though they are very different in spirit. I hadn't found myself then at all.

JM: So then you had Caroline – Cassie – and you and Vic set up as artists in your grandmother's house at Ericeira. Now, you say that was a blank period as far as your painting was concerned.

PR: I couldn't paint. I was stuck. So Vic said: 'Why don't you just draw'. So I drew and drew, things from my head mostly.

JM: But you were resolved to be an artist, there was no doubt of that.

PR: I'd made up my mind about that many years before at St Julian's, thanks to my teachers' encouragement. It seemed a natural thing to be. But at that time I was stuck. It was a very difficult time.

JM: It wasn't a problem both of you being artists.

PR: It never has been, never. I always regarded Vic to be so good, you see. I always admired his work so much. Also I needed help and Victor was always very generous about giving it. Never once did he not take the trouble to listen to me. Now, that has been the big bonus in my life, I guess, because I lived with a very intelligent and generous man in that respect. So, I've gained from it more than he has because I can't help him but he can help me. And that's it. I've always followed his advice.

JM: And now you've got a whole family of very talented artists. Did you teach them at all?

PR: Not really. Cassie always had a facility for making things, a tremendous ability. And Nick could always draw. We did draw together when he had his appendix out as a child and I was able to stay with him in hospital; but he already drew quite beautifully, quite naturally. And Vicky was always more literary.

JM: Then there was the first of the great releases in your life, you discovered Dubuffet.

PR: First I discovered Henry Miller. Oh, it was so terrific. I couldn't get at the dirty bits quick enough. Then I discovered Dubuffet. And that's the word – it released me. Whatever releases one about making art is beneficial. The exhibition was in London, and I was writing home these letters to Cassie with little childlike drawings at the foot of the page to illustrate what we were doing. And then I saw Dubuffet and I thought: 'This guy does what I do at the bottom of the letter big, right? And for real.' So I started doing my childlike scribbles big as well. It got me back in touch with being a kid again on the floor, in fact I began to work on a table, and play – and play.

JM: The release was from what?

PR: The release was from trying to do serious grown up art. That's where art school was bad for me. I was painting out there on an easel in the conventional way and I lost touch with this thing of being a kid. I had been doing a lot of portraits, rather expressionistic portraits, where the paint was very important and all that. I was describing something, but the drawings came direct from inside with nothing in between. They were direct from feeling to hand: that's it, feeling to hand. 'I started doing a painting a day. Very exciting.

JM: And then you got back to that doll – you started cutting up things, doing collages.

PR: Yes. I started cutting up magazines and then I found I couldn't get things I wanted from magazines so I started doing my own figures and cutting them up. I got a lot of pleasure cutting up; as you say, just like I did as a kid cutting up the baby's fingers. It's a masochistic thing, I think. And that gave rise to lots of images, one flowing from another, lots and lots and lots of images.

JM: And this first stage culminated in the collaged painting, 'The Dogs of Barcelona'.

PR: In a way. But the reason why 'The Dogs of Barcelona' is important is because it's the best painting, that's why. It has got a vitality and toughness about it, I think, that subsequently nothing else has for me. Well, maybe in a different way. While I did it I was overcome with emotion. It sounds ridiculous, but I got very excited doing it and then I felt ill because I was so excited. And I think that intensity shows, but it looks quite elegant now. It looked cruder then. Things do become more elegant in time.

JM: It was triggered off by a story in 'The Times'.

PR: The authorities in Barcelona decided there were too many stray dogs and they decided to get rid of them by chucking poisoned meat around in an indiscriminate, brutal, way. And I thought this reflected the political situation at the time in Spain and in Portugal, which was also brutally dictatorial. But it was straight out of my own experiences in the doing of it. The initial story just enables you to get in touch with your own stories.

JM: How did the political situation impinge on your life, on ordinary life?

PR: Always caution, caution, caution. Don't do it. Don't do it. Ridiculous.

JM: I don't think of you being a political activist, a dogmatist.

PR: I'm not now, but in Portugal you were very conscious of it, sure. My father always hoped that after the War, with a Labour Government in England, there would have been a change of attitude to Spain and Portugal but things went on just the same, England didn't care.

JM: Did your father like you being an artist?

PR: He was marvellous. He was financially supportive and understanding of everything. And he was really pleased that my first show was in Portugal. That was in 1965, six months before he died. He liked the pictures and it was a great success, like a party, amazing. He was proud of me. It was very nice.

JM: You were anxious he should be proud of you.

PR: I always wanted to prove that I was as good as a boy, that kind of thing. Because they were disappointed that I hadn't turned out to be a chap.

JM: Were they very disappointed?

PR: I think my grandmother was disappointed, and my father at first, but he got over it pretty quick.

JM: I ask because I wondered if it had contributed to the subversion of males that I detect in your pictures. Vic quotes you saying: 'Life is full of men making a grand gesture and falling on their arse.' Do you agree there's a little bit of a niggle there?

PR: Yes, maybe, but my father never did grand gestures. It's more to do with contradiction. You see, this is something that has always fascinated me. I can't get over the fact that somebody who is compassionate, understanding, can also be cruel, because of their own hang-ups. I don't get used to this, though it's pretty obvious. I mean, when you're a kid, you could be enjoying playing with somebody very much, and then slap them, and then kiss them to make it better. I mean you take pleasure in being cruel to people in a perverse sort of way. It's just something in one's nature, I guess. And these complicated things are endlessly fascinating, endlessly fascinating.

JM: You said you got your first show just in time for your father to see it and that it was a success, a boost. Could you say a bit more about it, about your artistic life in Portugal.

PR: The first time I showed my pictures at all in Portugal was at an open exhibition organized by The Gulbenkian Foundation in 1961. Each artist could submit three works, which I did, and they all got accepted. It was at the handing in for that show that Bartolomeu Cid dos Santos introduced me to Menez, who was to become a great friend; though it wasn't 'till two years later in London that we saw each other regularly. I love her recent work and am always expectant and full of curiosity when I visit her studio in Lisbon. In 1963

Menez introduced me to the poet Alberto de Lacerda, who had been living in London for some years. I think the success of my first individual show in Lisbon would not have been the same had I not met Alberto. The show came about when Fernando Pernes, who was the Director of the new Galeria de Arte Moderna in the Sociedade Nacional de Belas Artes, invited me to exhibit there. Alberto wrote the introduction and because he knew so many artists and painters I was able to invite them to the show. He's remained a close friend.

JM: The late 1960s and early 1970s were a less happy period for you: Vic was diagnosed to have multiple sclerosis, there was the Revolution, with which you were in sympathy but which was problematical in terms of the family business, and you were increasingly unhappy with your own work. Nonetheless there were fine pictures: 'The Punishment Room', 'The Martyr', 'The Green Dog'.

PR: 'The Punishment Room' was painted in my mother's house and brought all those memories of Mummies, Daddies and Grandpas. But the pictures become more forced, more wilful, I think that's the word, wilful. 'The Green Dog' was a good one, but it's unfeeling,. It's an accurate reflection of what I was like at the time, cold and brittle. As Vic says: 'The feelings are not so much expressed, as betrayed.' So being very unhappy and depressed, the pictures were not very nice. I became very depressed. I mean really badly depressed.

JM: By life in general, and then you began psychotherapy. Did that help?

PR: I think it helped by making me more myself, less distanced – which is very bad.

JM: How long did the therapy last?

PR: Like yesterday. I don't know. I stopped full-time about six years ago.

JM: And pictures began to come again.

PR: Well they never stopped, but they were repellent. 'The Chinese Bridge' I like. It's quite tough. It has begun to break out. It's less controlled. And then came 'The Annunciation', which is still very cramped, but it's got something.

JM: I remember you saying it was about the fear that Mary must have felt, the awfulness of her destiny; which was the aspect that interested you in Botticelli's version of the story. But it wasn't a breakthrough. The next big breakthrough, the next Dubuffet-like release, was just after this. And that was giving up collage in favour of drawing direct.

PR: That's right. Well, the process increasingly began to get

in the way again. If you have a clear idea of what's in your mind's eye, there's no trouble. It comes out in your hand. But if you don't quite know what you want to do and you look to the marks to suggest something – forget it.

JM: Was it a very sudden decision?

PR: Absolutely. It was another case of the right person at the right time. There was a Portuguese student at Chelsea – Joao Penalva. I met him through Vic's teaching there. We began to talk and got on well, so one day I showed him the pictures I was working on and he said: 'Why don't you do some just leaving them as they are, not cutting them up.' And it dawned on me, just as it had done with Dubuffet's scribbles, that this was what I had to do. He said this to me on Friday afternoon and I was so excited I couldn't wait for the weekend to be over, so I could get back to the studio and start. That was another release. I just drew and drew.

*   *   *

JM: There were the monkey series, the Operas, the Vivian Girls, 1984, all in acrylic on paper, all continuing the 'foot of the letter' method. Is there anything you'd like to add about them?

PR: I only drew the operas I'd seen with my father. The Vivian Girls were characters form a book by Henry Darger, an 'outsider' artist, who was recommended to me by Victor Musgrave. I never read the book, in fact, but a synopsis of it and it triggered off stories of my own invention. Darger's girls live on another planet ruled by very wicked soldiers, and they were always in bondage but thanks to their cunning pranks they were always getting the better of their captors.

JM: There was a gradual change from animal characters to humans, like the Vivian Girls, and now of course it's nothing but humans.

PR: I dropped the masks. But the invention is still in the drawing, like it always was. I still do lots of little drawings and I still work the first half of the big paintings on the floor.

JM: And they're still a lot to do with your childhood.

PR: My childhood or things happening in my life, of course.

JM: Another big difference is that you now set your characters in space and the figures are much larger. That must pose new problems.

PR: The drawings are from mind to hand and the pictures just make them more concrete that's all. Of course more complex things come into it. In pictures you can see things better. You have to find the right gesture, the right stance, expression on faces have to be right. I used to do things that were flying all over the page, because I wanted it to look like a page from a book; the whole story spread out like a book so that you can read it from left to right, top to bottom. But to make the figures three-dimensional I had to ground them, and that meant light and shade. I said to Vic: I don't know how to paint the floor.' And he said: "It's very easy. You do the object and when you make the shadow that makes the floor. 'Seeing the 'Northern Light' exhibition changed my painting a lot. It came at the right time. I mean, if I'd seen that show, like, four or five years ago, I wouldn't have looked at it twice.

JM: Masked or unmasked you have always had real people in mind haven't you.

PR: I usually have someone in mind but the faces are still masks in a way, Lila, who stays with us and helped nurse Vic, has been my model for most of the women in the recent pictures.

JM: You wrote: "My paintings are stories, but they are not narratives in that they have no past or future." And therefore everyone seeing the picture must make up their own story in front of it, must draw their own conclusions. Is that still true?

PR: Absolutely.

JM: But 'The Maids' is derived from a Genet play and has a very stagey setting. Do you see its characters in a play?

PR: In play.

JM: Not in a *play.*

PR: No. In play. They're all characters in play. Sweet.

JM: Nonetheless, I think it would be interesting to see one painting from your point of view; and I wonder therefore if you'd talk through 'The Cadet', which I know is currently your favourite of the paintings now in your studio. Like the others it is in acrylic on paper, which has then been stuck on canvas.

PR: Well, there wasn't any literary reference. It came to me as an image – bonk. So I did a drawing of it – two or three just to get the right position. I wanted the young man to be slightly younger than his sister, possibly thirteen and she'd be like fifteen, and she's more knowing than he is and he's depending on her quite a lot. I can't really explain it any more because the whole thing just came to me in one go.

JM: What about the surroundings?

PR: I very much wanted that avenue going up and disappearing into the distance, a bit like a theatrical backdrop. And the sky is meant to be like a sky from my catechism book. And then the props were very important. Her bag had to be brown like that, lined in red. I mean it had to be dangerous, as if it could snap shut. Both it and the gloves are like – I suppose it's pretty obvious – but like sex symbols. But opposites. And the cockerel is small and puffed up, and a pretend one, a porcelain one; so it shows he's impotent, the poor cadet. And it's a lesson you see – a lesson for us and also a lesson between the two of them. It's about accepting fate, you see. Accepting the way things are; in a nice sort of way. It's not an unhappy picture at all.

JM: What pleases you most about it?

PR: It's the wholeness of it – the way the figures are so compact, especially the girl crouched on the ground.

JM: You've been painting now for thirty years, do you find age and experience beneficial?

PR: Age is good. You concentrate much more, you focus much more on what you want to do. I have a grandchild and that's interesting too, because I find she reminds me much more of my childhood than the children did. Your own children are always too close to you, too much of a concern.

JM: Age is another release.

PR: I don't know about men, but I think it releases women a lot.

JM: You can say – and you know more – what you feel.

PR: That's been more of a problem for me in real life than in the pictures. No, when the pictures are going well you just can't wait for the next morning to come. And that's very good, a very good feeling. Painting is practical, but it's magical as well. Being in this studio is like being inside my own theatre.

44　**The Maids** 1987

42   **The Soldier's Daughter** 1987

43　**The Policeman's Daughter** 1987

46   **The Cadet and his Sister** 1988

47   **Departure** 1988

45   **The Family** 1988 (detail)

Left: 47   **Departure** 1988 (detail)

45   **The Family** 1988

Paula Rego

1935
Born in Lisbon
1945-51
Educated St Julian's School, Carcavelos
1952-56
The Slade School of Art
1957-63
Lived in Ericeira, Portugal with her husband the painter Victor Willing
1962-63
Bursary from the Gulbenkian Foundation, Lisbon
1963-75
Lived in London and Portugal
1976
Settled permanently in London
1983
Visiting Lecturer in Painting, Slade School of Art
1988
Retrospective Exhibition, Gulbenkian Foundation, Lisbon

One Person Exhibitions

1965
SNBA, Lisbon
1971
Galeria Sào Mamede, Lisbon
1972
Galeria Alvarez, Porto
1974
Galeria da Emenda, Lisbon
1975
Módulo, Centro Difusor da Arte, Lisbon
1977
Módulo Centro Difusor da Arte, Porto
1978
Galeria III, Lisbon
1981
AIR Gallery, London
1982
Galeria III, Lisbon; Edward Totah Gallery, London
1983
Arnolfini, Bristol; Galerie Espace, Amsterdam
1984
South Hill Park Arts Centre, Bracknell; Midland Group,
Nottingham; Edward Totah Gallery, London
1985
The Art Palace, New York; Edward Totah Gallery, London
1987
Selected work 1981-1986, Aberystwyth Arts Centre and tour;
Edward Totah Gallery, London
1988
Fundação Calouste Gulbenkian, Lisbon; Casa de Serralves, Porto

Group Exhibitions

1955

Young Contemporaries, London.

1961

Segunda Exposiçaõ de Artes Plásticas, Fundaçaõ Calouste Gulbenkian, Lisbon.

1965

Six Artists, Institute of Contemproary Arts, London.

1967

Bienal de Tokyo; *Novas Iconologias*, Lisbon; *Art Portugais – Peinture et sculpture de Naturalisme à nos jours*, Brussels, Paris, Madrid.

1969

Represented Portugal in the XI Bienal de Sào Paulo, Brazil; *Gravure Portugaise Contemporaine*, Paris.

1970

Novos Sintomas na pintura portuguesa, Galeria Judite Dacruz, Lisbon.

1973

Pintura portuguesa de hoje – abstractos e Neo-figurativos, Lisbon, Salamanca, Barcelona; *26 Artistas de Hoje*, Lisbon; *Exposição de Artistas Modernos Portugueses*, Galleria Quadrum, Lisbon.

1974

Expo AICA, SNBA.

1975

XIII Bienal de São Paulo; *Figuraçaõ Hoje?*, Lisbon.

1976

Arte Portugués Contemporanea, Galerie Nazionale d'Arte Moderna, Roma; *Art Portugais Contemporain*, Musée d'Art Contemporain de la Ville de Paris; *Exposição de Arte Moderna Portuguesa*, SNBA, Lisbon.

1977

Artistas Portugueses em Madrid – Pintura e Escultura Contemporaneas, Madrid.

1978

Portuguese Art since 1910, Royal Academy of Art, London; *Exposiçaõ individual*, Galeria III, Lisbon.

1979

Femina, UNESCO, Paris.

1981

Artists in Camden, Camden Arts Cetre, London; *Ante-visão do Centro de Art Moderna*, Fundação Çalouste Gulbenkian, Lisbon; *The Subjective Eye*, Midland Group, Nottingham.

1982

Three Women, Edward Totah Gallery, London; *Inner Worlds*, Midland Group, Nottingham; *Pintura portuguesa contemporânea*, Museu Luis de Camões, Macau; *Hayward Annual*, London; *John Moores Exhibition*, Liverpool.

1983

Third Biennale of Graphic Arts, Baden Baden; *Eight in the eighties*, New York; *Marathon 83*, New York.

1984

1984 – an exhibition, Camden Arts Centre, London; *Os Novos Primitivos*, Cooperative Arvore, Porto.

1985

The British Art Show, Ikon Gallery, Birmingham; *Diálogo sobre arte contemporânea*, Centro de Arte Moderna, Fundação Calouste Gulbenkian, Lisbon; Bienal de Paris; *Animals*, Edward Totah Gallery, London; *Exposição Diálogo*, Fundação Calouste Gulbenkian, Lisbon; John Moores Exhibition, Liverpool; Bienal de Sào Paulo (representing Britain); *Passion and power*, La Mama and Gracie Mansion, New York.

1986

A primeira década, Módulo – Centro Difusor da Arte, Lisboa; *Le XXéme au Portugal*, Centre Albert Borchette, Brussels; *Terceira Exposição de Artes Plásticas*, Fundação Calouste Gulbenkian, Lisbon-AICA-PHILAE, SNBA, Lisbon; *Love Sacred and Profane*, Plymouth; *The Human Zoo*, Nottingham Castle Museum, Nottingham; *Contemporary British and Malaysian Art*, National Gallery, Kuala Lumpur; *Nove – Nine Portuguese Painters*, John Hansard Gallery, Southampton.

1987

Art Contemporáneo Portugués, Madrid; *Current Affairs – British Painting and Sculpture in the 1980s*, Museum of Modern Art, Oxford, Hungary, Poland and Czechoslovakia; *70-80: Arte Portugusa*, Brasilia, Sào Paulo, Rio de Janeiro; *Alberto da Lacerda – O Mundo de um poeta*, Fundação Calouste Gulbenkian, Lisbon; *30 Obras de Arte União de Bancos Portugeses*, Casa de Serralves, Porto; *Feira do Circo*, Forum Picoas Lisbon; *Exposiçao Amadeo Souza-Cardoso*, Casa de Serralves, Porto; *Obras de uma Colecçao Particular*, Casa de Serralves, Porto.

1988

Works on Paper by contemporary artists, Marlborough Fine Art, London; *35 Pinturas de Colecção do Banco Português do Atlântico*, Casa de Serralves, Porto; *Cries and Whispers*, British Council Travelling Exhibition, Australia; *Narrative paintings*, Castlefield Gallery, Manchester; *Objects and Image, Aspects of British Art in the 1980's*, Stoke-on-Trent Art Gallery.

Bibliography

Catalogues

Alberto de Lacerda: 'Fragmentos de um poema intitulado Paula Rego', *Paula Rego,* SNBA, Lisbon, 1965.

Paula Rego Expoê, Galeria São Mameda, Lisbon, 1971.

Victor Willing: 'Paula Rego', *Paula Rego: Paintings 1982-3,* Arnolfini, Bristol; Galerie Espace, Amsterdam 1983.

Lynne Cooke: 'Paula Rego', *Paula Rego: Paintings 1984-5,* Edward Totah Gallery, London, 1985.

Alistair Hicks: 'Paula Rego', *Paula Rego: Selected Work 1981-1986,* Aberystwyth Arts Centre.

Paula Rego: Girl and Dog, Edward Totah Gallery, London, 1987.

Paula Rego, Fundação Calouste Gulbenkian, 1988.

Il Exposicão de Artes Plásticas, Fundação Calouste Gulbenkian, Lisbon, 1961.

Victor Willing: *Six Artists,* Institute of Contemporary Art, London, 1965.

Art Portugais – Peinture et Sculpture de Naturalisme à nos jours, Brussels, 1967.

Esposição Colectiva, Galeria S. Mamede, Lisbon, 1972.

Salette Tavares: "A Estrutura Semântica na obra de Paula Rego, *Expo AICA,* SNBA, Lisbon, 1974.

Hellmut Wohl: *Portuguese Art since 1910,* London, Royal Academy of Art, 1978.

Deanna Petherbridge: 'Nineteen eighty four in 1984', *1984 – An Exhibition,* Camden Arts Centre, London 1984.

Alexander Moffat: 'Retrieving the Image', *The British Art Show,* Arts Council of Great Britain.

Nine Portuguese Painters, John Hansard Gallery, Southampton, 1986.

70-80 Arte Portuguesa, Brasilia, São Paulo, Rio de Janeiro, 1987.

Lewis Biggs and David Elliott: *Current Affairs,* Museum of Modern Art, Oxford 1987.

Feira do Circo, Forum Picoas, Lisbon, 1987.

Works on paper by contemporary artists, Marlborough Fine Art, London, 1988.

Lewis Biggs: ' A context for the exhibitions', *Cries and Whispers,* British Council 1988.

Articles
1961

Andrew Forge: The Slade – to the present day, *MOTIF Magazine,* Spring.

1965

Alberto de Lacerda: 'Paula Rego nas belas Artes', *Diàrio de Notícias,* Lisbon, 25 December.

Nelson di Maggio: 'O Medo Criador'. *Jornal de Letras e Arte,* 29 December.

1966

Fernando Pernes: 'Entrevista com Paula Rego': 'A minha pintura não é nêo-dada', *Jornal de Letras e Artes*, Lisbon 5 January.
Salette Tavares: 'Excerto do poema em três tempos de Pedro Sete – para Paula Figueiroa Rego', *Diário de Noticias*, 10 February.
Keith Sutton: 'Paula Rego: Every picture tells a story', *London Life*, 19 March.

1971

Victor Willing: 'The Imagiconography of Paula Rego', *Colóquio*, April, pp. 43-49.
Eurico Gonçalves: 'Paula Rego: Naõ é cola que faz a colagam, *Flama*, 4 June.

1974

Salette Tavares: 'Dados para uma leitura de Paula Rego', *Expresso*, 2 July.

1981

John McEwen: 'Telling Tales', *The Spectator*, 30 May.
Waldemar Janusczak: 'Paula Rego/Ronald Boyd', *The Guardian*, 2 June.
John McEwen: 'Paula Rego', *Colóquio Artes*, No. 23 (50), September, pp. 58-59.

1982

José Luis Porfíro: 'Os monstros no castelo da pureza', *Expresso*, 3 April.
Waldemar Janusczak: 'Hammering the Nail on the Head', *The Guardian*, 8 May.
Sarah Kent: *Time Out*, 10-16 September.
John McEwen: 'Triangles', *The Spectator*, 11 September.
Richard Cork: 'The beast in us all', *The Standard*, 16 September.
Andrea Hill: 'Paula Rego, *Artscribe*, No. 37, October, pp. 33-37.

1983

John McEwen: 'Rego/Willing', *Art in America*, February.
Bernado Pinto de Almeida: 'Vida e Operas de Paula Rego', *Jornal de Letras*, 26 April.
John Russell: 'Eight in the Eighties', *New York Times*, 20 May.

1984

Caroline Collier: 'Paula Rego: Art from inside', *Studio International*, Vol. 197, No. 1007, p. 56.

1985

Susan Gill: 'Paula Rego' –, *Artnews*, NY, October.
Alistair Hicks: 'Mischief in Paradise', *The Spectator*, 7 September.
William Feaver: 'Quack, quack here', *The Observer*, London, 15 September.
Mary Rose Beaumont: 'Paula Rego', *Arts Review* London, 27 September.
Sarah Kent: *Time Out*, 19-25 September, pp. 3-29.
F. T. Castle: 'Paula Rego', *Art in America*', December, p. 126.

1987

Mary Rose Beaumont: 'Paula Rego', *Arts Review*, London, March.
William Packer: 'Current British artists show their strengths', *The Financial Times*, London 3 March.
Sarah Kent: *Time Out*, 11-18 March.
Michael Phillipson: 'Paula Rego', *Artscribe International*.
William Feaver: 'Shy Venus, Earth Mother', *The Observer*, 22 March.
Lynne Cooke: 'Paula Rego', *Flash Art*, no. 134, May.
Alexandre Melo Joao Pinharanda: 'Paula Rego Tudo o que pinto vem de Portugal', *Jornal de Letras*, 15 June.
John McEwen: 'Paula Rego at Totah', *Art in America*, July, pp. 37-48.
Andrew Graham Dixon: 'Painters for the Eighties', *The Independent*, London, 1 July.

1988

Judith Higgins: 'Painted Dreams', *American Art News*, vol 87 No. 2, February.
Alexadre Melo: 'O Mundo Magico de Paula Rego', *Expresso*, 7 May.
Joao Pinharanda: 'Paula Rego: As Meninas Exemplares', *J.L.* 10 May.
Jose Luis Porfino: 'Paula Rego – A distancia do medo', *Expresso*, 21 May.
Jill Joliffe: 'Shades of Youth', *The Guardian*, 30 May.
Germaine Greer: 'Paula Rego', *Modern Painters*, Vol. 1, No. 3, Autumn.

List of Works

1
Birthday Party 1953
Oil on canvas
124 × 205cm
Private collection

2
Portrait of a Lady 1959
Mixed media on canvas
73 × 100cm
Collection: Rui Pocas

3
The Eating 1959
Collage/Oil on canvas
95 × 113cm
Collection: Francisco Pereira Coutinho

4
Persephone 1959
Oil on canvas
100 × 140cm
Collection: Mac-Porto

5
Salazar a Vomitar a Pátria 1960
(Salazar Vomiting the Homeland)
Oil on canvas
94 × 120cm
Collection: Centro de Arte Moderna/Fundação Calouste
Gulbenkian, Lisbon

6
Proverb 1961
Collage/Oil on canvas
96.5 × 123.5cm
Private collection

7a
Travelling Circus 1960
Oil on paper
30 × 40cm
Private collection

7b
Trophy 1960
Oil on paper
29 × 42cm
Private collection

7c
Order has been Established . . . 1961
Oil on paper
41.5 × 47.5cm
Private collection

7d
Untitled 1961
Oil on paper
22 × 31cm
Private collection

7e
Untitled 1961
Oil on paper
22 × 30cm
Private collection

7f
Long Live Ding-Dong 1961
Oil on paper
24 × 35cm
Private collection

7g
Always at your Excellency's Service 1961
Oil on paper
22.5 × 25cm
Private collection

8
When we had a House in the Country 1961
Collage/Oil on canvas
49.5 × 144.5cm
Collection: the artist

9
Aurora Latina 1962
Collage/Oil on canvas
72.5 × 92cm
Collection: Alberto de Lacerda

10
Snow 1964
Collage/Oil on canvas
68 × 92cm
Private collection

11
Centaur 1964
Collage/Oil on canvas
140 × 139cm
Private collection

12
Stray Dogs (The Dogs of Barcelona) 1965
Collage/Oil on canvas
160 × 185cm
Collection: Francisco Pereira Coutinho

13
Julieta 1965
Collage/Oil on canvas
152 × 183cm
Private collection

14
Regicide 1965
Collage/Oil on canvas
150 × 200cm
Private collection

15
Red Monkey beats his Wife 1981
Acrylic on paper
69 × 105cm
Collection: the artist

16
Wife cuts off Red Monkey's Tail 1981
Acrylic on paper
68 × 101cm
Collection: Waldemar Janusczak

17
Red Monkey offers Bear a Poisoned Dove 1981
Acrylic on paper
69 × 105cm
Collection: C. Willing

18
**The Bear, The Bear's Wife and Son play with
The Red Monkey** 1981
Acrylic on paper
69 × 105cm
Collection: Dr Mario Soares, Lisbon

19
Monkey Drawing 1982
Acrylic on paper
76 × 57cm
Nicola Jacobs Gallery, London

20
Pregnant Rabbit Telling Her Parents 1982
Acrylic on paper
103 × 141cm
Edward Totah Gallery, London

21
Rabbit and weeping Cabbage 1982
Acrylic on paper
103 × 141cm
Edward Totah Gallery, London

22
Cabbage and Potato 1982
Acrylic on paper
103 × 142cm
Collection: Irwin Joffe

23
Going Out 1982
Acrylic on paper
102 × 136cm
Collection: Deborah and Peter Tyler

24
Samurai 1982
Acrylic on paper
156 × 215cm
Private collection

25
La Boheme 1983
Acrylic on paper
240 × 203cm
Collection: the artist

26
Aida 1983
Acrylic on paper
72.5 × 92cm
Collection: the artist

27
Rigoletto 1983
Acrylic on paper
240 × 203cm
Collection: the artist

28
The Girl of the Golden West 1983
Acrylic on paper
240 × 203cm
Collection: the artist

29
The Pig's Secret 1984
Acrylic on paper
242 × 179cm
Edward Totah Gallery, London

30
On the Beach 1985
Acrylic on canvas
200 × 220cm
Collection: the artist

31
The Bride 1985
Acrylic on canvas
220 × 200cm
Collection: Roger and Cathy Willis

32
Untitled 'Girl & Dog' series 1986
Acrylic on paper
112 × 76cm
Collection: The British Council

33
Untitled 'Girl & Dog' series 1986
Acrylic on paper
112 × 76cm
Private collection

34
Untitled 'Girl & Dog' series 1986
Acrylic on paper
112 × 76cm
Collection: Vanessa Devereux

35
Untitled 'Girl & Dog' series 1986
Acrylic on paper
112 × 76cm
Collection: Robin Woodhead and Mary Allen

36
Untitled Girl & Dog series 1986
Acrylic on paper
112 × 76cm
Collection: Neville Shulman

37
Girl lifting up her Skirts to a Dog 1986
Acrylic on paper
80 × 60cm
Edward Totah Gallery, London

38
Prey 1986
Acrylic on paper/canvas
150 × 150cm
Collection: Richard Salmon, London

39
Two Girls and a Dog 1987
Acrylic on paper/canvas
150 × 150cm
Private collection

40
The Little Murderess 1987
Acrylic on paper/canvas
150 × 150cm
Collection: Robert and Rebecca Lilley

41
Looking Back 1987
Acrylic on paper/canvas
150 × 150cm
Saatchi Collection, London

42
The Soldier's Daughter 1987
Acrylic on paper/canvas
213.4 × 152.4cm
Marlborough Fine Art, London

43
The Policeman's Daughter 1987
Acrylic on paper/canvas
213.4 × 152.4cm
Saatchi Collection, London

44
The Maids 1987
Acrylic on paper/canvas
213.4 × 243.9cm
Saatchi Collection, London

45
The Family 1988
Acrylic on paper/canvas
213.4 × 213.4cm
Saatchi Collection, London

46
The Cadet and his Sister 1988
Acrylic on paper/canvas
213.4 × 213.4cm
Marlborough Fine Art, London

47
Departure 1988
Acrylic on paper/canvas
213.4 × 152.4cm
Collection: the artist